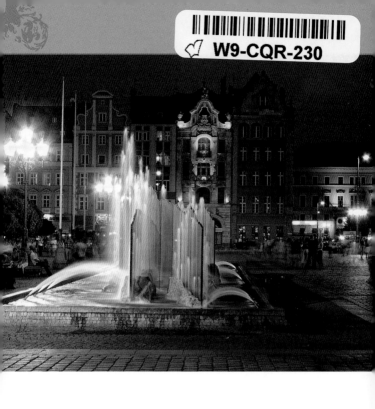

WROCŁAW
guidebook

POLSKA

Szczecin

Berlin

Poznań

Warszawa

DEUTSCHLAND

E261

E36

WROCŁAW

E40 — E40 — E40 — E67

Łódź

Dresden

E67

E40

Praha — E67

Kraków

ČESKÁ REPUBLIKA

E462

Ostrava

E65
E50

Brno

SLOVENSKO

Wien

Bratislava

ÖSTERREICH

Text: Marta Miniewicz, Magdalena Irek-Koszerna

Photos: Małgorzata Bełdowska, Anna Iwaniuk,
Adam Marecik, Dominik Ptak, Paweł Syposz, Marcin Hubicki,
Magdalena Irek-Koszerna, Maciej Pieńkowski
the publisher's archive ZET

Typeset and graphic design: Anna Iwaniuk, FeliX

Maps: FeliX

Translation: Wojciech Wojtasiewicz

© Wydawnictwo ZET* Wrocław 2011
All rights reserved
tel. +48 71 793 67 47
fax +48 71 783 28 64
e-mail: biuro@wydawnictwozet.pl
www.wydawnictwozet.pl
ISBN: 978-83-62013-19-7

The astronomical clock on the eastern façade of the Town Hall

Wrocław is a dynamically developing capital of Lower Silesia. It is the fourth biggest city in Poland taking into consideration its population where ca. 640 thousand people live on the area of 293 km². Wrocław is a scientific and economic centre of the whole region. It is a full of vitality academic and cultural centre.

Wrocław – the city of meetings

During the Eucharist Congress in 1997 Pope John Paul II called Wrocław "a city of meetings", "a city that unites". In Wrocław, "a microcosm of Europe" various traditions, religions and cultures have met and joined together. Among cultural events taking place in Wrocław it is worth mentioning, among other: Actor's Song Festival, International Festival "Wratislavia Cantans" – Music and Fine Arts, International Meetings of the Open Theatre, International Biennale of Media Art – "WRO", Brave Festival, Film Festival "Era – New Horizons" and superproductions of Wrocław Opera Theatre.

Ostrów Tumski panorama

▨ Wrocław – the city of the youth

Each sixth inhabitant of Wrocław is a student. There are 22 universities present in Wrocław with almost 140 thousand students learning at them. University of Wrocław can be found in the list of 500 best universities in the world.

▨ Wrocław – the city of greenery

The Old City in Wrocław is surrounded by a belt of greenery – the Old City Promenade. The city boasts of its 44 parks of which the biggest are: Szczytnicki Park (Park Szczytnicki) with the area of 100ha and Zachodni Park (Western Park) with its 75ha. Within the city there are woodland areas. Las Rędziński (Rędziny Wood) with 400ha contains the oldest tree growing in Wrocław, i.e. a 470-year-old oak-tree.

▨ Wrocław – the city of bridges

Wrocław is called "Venice of the North". More than 100 bridges and footbridges span over the Odra and its tributaries, the city moat and river canals join 12 islands with the mainland.

▨ Wrocław – the city of Gothic churches

The panorama of the city is marked by slender towers of Gothic churches. The most beautiful medieval churches are: the cathedral of St. John the Baptist, the Holy Cross church, the church of Our Lady on Piasek, St. Elisabeth's church, St. Mary Magdalene's church, the church of Sts Wenceslas, Stanislaus and Dorothy in the Old City; the city register of architectural relics contains almost 3000 sacral and lay objects.

Wrocław coats of arms

Wrocław coats of arms dates from 1530. The new coats of arms was given to the city in Prague by King Ferdinand I. The symbols of Wrocław coats of arms depicts the rich history of the city:

■ a white Czech lion supported on two paws with a crown on its head placed against a red background is a symbol of The Czech Kingdom, within which Wrocław was situated from 1335, i.e. after the Wrocław Piasts dying out;

■ a black eagle with a crescent, white band on the chest against a golden background is a Silesian eagle, a coats of arms of Wrocław Piasts, recognized as a coats of arms of Wrocław Duchy;

■ St. John the Evangelist, a figure against a red background, has been a patron of the city council and the Town Hall chapel since the 14th century;

■ The letter "w" against a golden background is an initial of the official, Latin name of the city, Wratislavia;

■ The head of St. John the Baptist on a bowl in the central part of the shield is a symbol of the first patron of Wrocław.

The mosaic on the Main Market Square floor; the biggest image of Wrocław coats of arms in the city, placed here in 1997 after the great flood which happened in the city

The city patrons

■ St. John the Baptist – the patron of Wrocław cathedral; he appears on the first city stamps, it is in the heart of Wrocław coats of arms; it is on the 24th of June that Wrocław celebrates its day.

■ St. Hedwig of Silesia – a Silesian patron, came from the Andechs family, the wife of Prince Henry the Bearded; she was buried in the church in Trzebnica; on the 14th of October Trzebnica sanctuary becomes a target of Lower Silesian pilgrims.

■ Bl. Czesław – he was announced the main patron of the city in 1963; he was the first prior of the Dominicans in Wrocław, the chapel under his name and his sarcophagus are in St Adalbert's church; according to a legend he saved the inhabitants of the city from the Mogul invasion in 1241.

■ St. Edith Stein – a patron of the United Europe; she was born and brought up in Wrocław in a Jewish family; she converted herself into Catholicism taking the name of Teresa Benedicta of the Cross; a doctor of philosophy; died in Auschwitz.

St. John the Baptist; a figure on the Tumski Bridge

The family house of Edith Stein, Nowowiejska Street 38; a seat of Culture Dialogue centre run by Edith Stein Society

St. Hedwig of Silesia; a statue on the Tumski Bridge

History of Wrocław

1000 – founding a bishopric in Wrocław by Boleslaus the Brave

1241 – the first location of the city, giving the Magdeburg law and the beginning of territory self-government

1335 – according to the will of Henry VI, the last Piast prince, the city was incorporated into the Czech Crown

1526 – after the death of King Louis the Jagiellon the city goes under the rule of Austrian Habsburgs

1702 – signing the foundation bill and creating the Jesuit Academy, Leopoldinum, by Emperor Leopold I

1741 – the beginning of Silesian wars, taking the city by Prussian army and going under the rule of the Hohenzollerns

1807 – taking the city by Napoleon's army; an to demolish the city walls

1811 – founding the University of Wrocław created from joining the Viadrina from Frankfurt on the Odra and the Jesuit Academy

1944 – the city is proclaimed a Keep – Festung Breslau

1945 – as a result of war the city was destroyed in 70%, incorporating Lower Silesia with Wrocław into Poland

1948 – The Exhibition of the Regained Lands and the World Congress of Intellectuals in Defence of Peace

1990 – the first democratic elections for the City Council of Wrocław

1997 – the 46th International Eucharistic Congress with the participation of Pope John Paul II; in July a tragic flood called the millennium flood

2000 – ceremonious celebrations of Wrocław Millennium

2005 – The European Summit of Regions and European Cities

Wrocław info coffee2go

Wrocław info coffee2go

Make friends with Wrocław

Welcome to Tourist and Cultural Information Centre

It is an innovative idea for promotion of local culture and artistic works, and propagating it among the citizens of Wrocław and the tourists who visit us. We are open to cooperation with local organizations which promote artistic works, galleries, clubs, community centres, and the artists themselves. We offer exchange of cultural information and free exposition of promotional materials.

In the Wrocław Info centre you can:
• get information about the current cultural events in our city • buy tickets for domestic and foreign cultural events • buy CDs of Wrocław's music bands • buy gadgets and souvenirs from Wrocław book accommodation • have a delicious frothy coffee

Opening hours (the whole week):
During the season (April the 1st until October the 31st), Mon-Fri 8.00 to 19.00 / Sat, Sun 9.00–20.00
Sukiennice St 12, 50-107 Wrocław, tel: +48 71 342 01 85, fax: +48 71 342 28 98, mobile: +48 605 222 227
e-mail: info@itwroclaw.pl, **www.wroclaw-info.pl**

Wrocław the meeting point

Come... Visit... See For Yourself...

Welcome to Tourist Information Centre!

Welcome to Tourist Information Centre „The Meeting Point" in Wrocław - a pleasant place for everyone. TIC staff offers help and advice in many different situations.

Tourist Information Centre helps with:
• choosing the most attractive places worth visiting, from a wide range of tourist attractions in the city and the region • booking accommodation.
In the Tourist Information Centre you can:
• find information materials • hire a Wrocław guide • buy tourist publications and keepsakes • buy gadgets and souvenirs from Wrocław • hire a bicycle or rent a car.

Opening hours (the whole week):
During the season (April the 1st until October the 31st), 9.00–21.00 outside the season 9.00–20.00
Rynek 14, 50-101 Wrocław, tel: +48 71 344 31 11, fax: +48 71 344 29 62, mobile: +48 663 888 725
e-mail: info@itwroclaw.pl, **www.wroclaw-info.pl**

Hardworking "Syzyfki" in Świdnicka Street

A dwarf image of the city

Looking at the streets of the Old City today one may think that a wave of fairy world immigrants flowed over us. Although there a bit of truth in it one must admit that dwarfs have lived in Wrocław for centuries. Recently they have become more courageous to come out from underground and show themselves to our "human" reality.

It is true, however, that they might have been encountered in Wrocław before, e.g. when they supported the Movement of the Orange Alternative openly. The proof of their participation is DWARF FATHER standing at the Świdnickie Pass, the old place of the leader's of the Orange Alternative Movement, Major Frydrych's happenings. That, however, is only history now. New times have come for dwarfs. They do not need to be hidden but, quite the contrary, one may have an impression that they are keen on being seen. It happens that some of them shoot between our legs in an easygoing and reckless way, as if they were not afraid that some of us would trip

On the Main Market Square and in its vicinity one can usually meet:

against them.

SŁUPNIKI – to notice them one should perk one's head as they live on lampposts;

GRAJEK AND MELOMAN – two inseparable mates spending whole nights and days between a flower shop and wedding dresses shop in Oławska Street;

GOŁĘBNIK – as the dove mail messenger he always lands on one of the sills of Spiż;

SYZYFKI – two workaholics, pushing balls along the pavement of Świdnicka Street next to the entrance to the post office;

ŻYCZLIWEK – always smiling, he usually stands leaning against a fountain and celebrating his name-day particularly pompously with the whole Wrocław on the European Day of warm-heartedness, always on the 21st of November;

OBIEŻYSMAK – he has a habit of sitting at the entrance to Pizza Hut restaurant at the Main Market Square;

PIEROŻNIK – he crouched at the entrance to STP, a restaurant in Kuźnicza Street;

KUŹNIK – he stands leaning against the wall of Kruk jeweller's shop, on the corner of Kuźnicza and Wita Stwosza Streets;

DRYNDEK – he chose the tenement house at 35 Main Market Square, where there is the seat of Dialog Telephone Company

One can give more and more names and it is impossible to give a closed list. The family of dwarfs has been growing and unveiling its new brother-dwarfs to notice whom one should only be watchful and perceptive.

"Turysta" – you will meet him in the Main Market Square at the Tourist Information Point

OLD CITY

OLD CITY

The northern architecture of the Main Market Square

1 The Main Market Square

"All the roads lead to..." the main market square in Wrocław. As many as 11 streets will lead us from various places in the city to one of the biggest medieval squares in Europe (the area of 3.7ha) which was demarcated already in the 13th century. Formerly it was the main market square in the city and now it vibrates with life due to other reasons. Dozens of restaurants and cafes, summer gardens and numerous events and open air concerts attract people of Wrocław and tourists. During the days of the city, a one-week festival, one can join a common breakfast eaten at the market and welcome the New Year together with others during a New year Eve's party.

"Seven Electors" tenement house, n°8 the Main Market Square

THE MAIN MARKET SQUARE

The Main Market Square – the so-called "Dove Square" – in the background the New Town Hall, the seat of the City Office in Wrocław

The market square is surrounded by historic tenement houses at its four sides. In 1945 a considerable number of houses were destroyed or partially damaged. Rebuilt after the war they amaze with a variety of architectural styles. One can see a mannerist style tenement building "The Griffons" (n°2), which houses a restaurant on its several levels (the cellars go down to 12 metres under the ground). The wall paintings on the Baroque house "Seven Electors" gave the name to the whole western side of the market. A surprising skyscraper from the end of the 1920s is a memory of, fortunately, an unrealised idea of rebuilding the market square into a modern financial centre of the city. The Modernist house of the Barasch brothers from 1904, nowadays "Phoenix"(Feniks) (n°31/32) was one of the first modern department houses in Wrocław.

The middle of the square is taken by the mid-square block, cut by several small streets. In the Przejście Żelaźnicze (Iron Pass) in the years 1965-1984 there was Laboratorium Theatre of Jerzy Grotowski. Beside the Old Town Hall situated at the southern side there is a 19th

The entrance to the Old Town Hall and the Museum of Townsmen's Art housed inside

century New Town Hall, the current seat of the president and the city authorities. A mini-brewery and "Spiż" restaurant with an interesting interior design were created in its cellars where you can taste a few types of beer and learn about the process of production of that drink that has been the most beverage in Wrocław forcenturies.

On the small square in front of the main entrance to the Town Hall there is a statue of Alexander Fredro, a Polish comedy playwright, and on the eastern side you can see the Wrocław pillory, a favourite place of meetings and the orienteering point nowadays and a place of shame in the past. For a few centuries public punishment has been executed here. During 50 years of the 15th century Wrocław assessors sentenced as many as 300 people to death. Lashing and tying to the pillory were punishments for minor crimes, e.g. for slandering a neighbour.

The statue of Alexander Fredro by Leonard Marconi (1897) brought to Wrocław from Lvov

The eastern, the richest Town Hall façade depicting, among other, scenes from medieval Wrocław townsmen's life

2 The Town Hall

"Wonderfully beautiful!" – these were the words of a Polish writer, Józef Ignacy Kraszewski. Wrocław Town Hall belongs undoubtedly to the most interesting and most valuable, lay Gothic-Renaissance historic sights of Middle Europe. Built from the end of the 13th century it was extended and rebuilt in the following centuries and played the role of the seat of the city authorities for a few hundred years. Its historic interiors house the Museum of Townsfolk Art with a Gallery of Famous Wrocław Inhabitants. Important official ceremonies take place in the representative Great Hall called the Knights' Hall.

The southern façade of the Town Hall amazes with an abundance of details. When we look at it more closely we can discern astonishing scenes among plant tangles hewn in stone: a drunk woman taken away on a cart, knights' jousting tournaments, St. George killing a dragon, heroes of Aesop's fables: a stork visiting a cunning fox. In the middle there is an entrance to the oldest inn in Wrocław – Piwnica Świdnicka (Świdnica Cellar). All of those who have visited Wrocław have visited the cellar. The inscription inside

The Town Hall – the eastern façade with the astronomical clock

The entrance to Świdnicka Cellar, the oldest inn in the city

the inn said: "The one who has not been in Piwnica Świdnicka has not been to Wrocław." In the 14th and the 15th centuries the famous beer from Świdnica was served there. Nowadays one can drink only the beer called Biały (White) and Czarny (Black) Ram. Above the entrance there are sculptures of a drunk farm-hand and a furious woman holding a clog in her hand. The scene is a warning against the consequences awaiting fanatic beer lovers after coming back home.

The middle part of the façade from the east holds an astronomical clock depicting moon phases. It is surrounded by Egyptian symbols of seasons. Sentences of Wrocław jury used to be announced from the bay window of the first floor (the old town hall chapel).

The western façade of the Town Hall with the 44-metre-high tower

THE SALT SQUARE

Wrocław flower stalls on the Salt Square

3   The Salt Square

It was demarcated during the first location of the city as an auxiliary market square. The square was designed for salt trade which was originally sold in 12 wooden sheds. Although the square was used to trade honey, wax and leather from Małopolska as well, it owes its name to salt merchandised there.

In 1453 John of Capistrano preached from one of the houses – an inquisitor and a famous preacher, a co-founder of the Bernardine Order, OFM. With his oratorical talent he persuaded Wrocław inhabitants to bring articles of luxury and sin to the Salt Square. The townsmen, being under the influence of his fervent speech and manifesting their spiritual change, burnt all the brought things on a stake.

The most imposing building at the Salt Square is the so-called Old Exchange (Stara Giełda) (n°16). It was designed by Karl Ferdinand Langhans and it refers to a Roman palace with its appearance. The main entrance is decorated with a magnificent Corinthian balcony portico and the topping of the first floor is surrounded by a chain of floral garlands and eagles. The building owes such an imposing outlook to Wrocław merchants, who wanted to underline their posi-

The Old Trade House on the Salt Square

tion in the city by a scale of the investment at the beginning of the 19th century.

In 1827 a statue of the Commander–in–Chief of the Prussian army from the times of Napoleon wars, a field marshal, Gebhard Leberecht Blücher was placed in the central point of the square changing the name of the square into Blücherplatz. The name functioned until 1947. A very modern looking tenement house "The Black Boy" (n°2/3) originated in the years 1925-1928 at the place of two other houses. The neighbouring house of the Oppenheimer Foundation (n°4) is the only wholly preserved Baroque house from the middle of the 18th century.

Nowadays, however, Wrocław flower girls are the most important at the square. At any time of the day and night one can buy a bunch of fresh flowers from them.

The Salt Square, a stone needle designed by A. Wyspiański, 1997

The Orthodox Cathedral of the Most Holy Mother of God's Birth

Evangelic-Augsburg church of God's Providence

The Mutual Respect District

In Wrocław, there are four churches neighbouring each other within the radius of only a few hundred metres that belong to four religious communities: Roman-Catholic, Orthodox, Evangelical-Augsburg and Jewish. At the meeting in 1995, in which representatives of all those communities took part, an idea of mutual co-operation without religious divisions was created. Ecumenical events and concerts take place in the District of Mutual Respect. No other place in the city realizes the idea of Wrocław as a meeting place of various traditions, religions and cultures in a more visible way.

The Church of the Lord's Providence in Kazimierza Wielkiego Street was built in the middle of the 18th century to the order of Frederick II the Great as the Court Church. It was the first church of Evangelical-Augsburg Church in Wrocław. Currently it belongs to the Lutherans. From the outside the building is in a Classicist style while inside it keeps a late Baroque interior design which is an ideal example of reformed churches interior design. The interior is an elliptical room with a double floor of galleries and a lectern altar.

The synagogue "The White Stork" in Włodkowica Street is a work of a famous architect, Karl Ferdinand Langhans. The work on its construction finished in 1829. It represents the Classicist style with a traditionally oriented longitudinal axis. The structure did not suffer much during World War II. Since

1989, after taking over the building by a Jewish community there have been actions to bring the temple back to its former splendour as while being un-used in the post-war years it was gradually going into ruin. Each last Saturday of the month there are Havdalah concerts and concerts within the frames of lots of Wrocław music festivals in the synagogue; there is an active choir attached to the synagogue as well.

The Catholic Baroque church of St. Anthony's is situated on a small parcel among dense architecture of the street called after the patron of the church. The hall-gallery church, built in the years 1685-1692 by a Wrocław master stonemason, Mateusz Bitner, to the design of an Italian architect, has genuine Baroque interior outfit. The church was erected by Franciscan monks after whom the monastery and the church were taken by St. Elisabeth's Sisters and after the war it was inhabited by the Salesians. Nowadays the spiritual service is held by Pauline fathers. It was already on the 13th of May 1945 that the first Holy Mass in Wrocław was served in that church.

The Roman-Catholic church of St. Anthony's

Nowadays the Chair of The Autocephalous Church of Poland in St. Nicolas Street is the former St. Barbara's Church. In its 700-hundred years history it was a Catholic, Evangelical and since 1963 an Orthodox church. The interiors under a Gothic vault hide a typical iconostas for the Orthodox Church and another contemporary one, a work of art of Jerzy Nowosielski, stained glass referring to Byzantine style and icons.

"The White Stork" synagogue

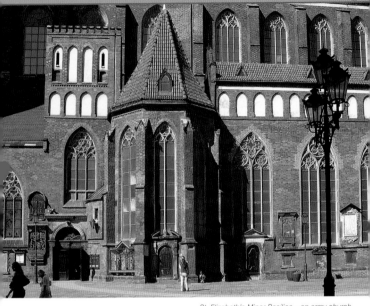

St. Elizabeth's Minor Basilica – an army church

8 St. Elisabeth's Church

The church situated near the Main Market Square is one of the biggest and most important churches of the left-bank Wrocław. The patron of the church built in stages from the beginning of the 14th century was St. Elizabeth of Hungary, a niece of St. Hedwig, the patron of Silesia. The church was a place of prayer and a burial place of the representatives of the wealthiest and the most important families of Wrocław townsmen. The burial and epitaph plates found in the outside walls of the church and in the middle of the church are its most precious treasure. In the southern aisle of the church there is a truly royal tomb of Heinrich Rybisch, who, according to a legend, used the Knights of the Cross with the Red Star abbot's passion for gambling and won the church from him playing dice. From that time (1525) the church became the main Protestant church in Silesia. Catholic faithful could not come to terms with the loss of such a beautiful church. When in 1529 a fierce storm went over Wrocław, as a result of which the helm of the church tower fell down to the ground, they recognized it as the heaven's plague for converting the confession. The Protestants commemorated that

Illumination on St. Elizabeth's Church tower

The nave in St. Elizabeth's Church

event (one can find a bas-relief on the church tower) commenting it in a totally different way. It was acknowledged that God holds the Protestant church in His care as nothing happened to anyone due to the disaster (the only victim was a black cat that was killed).

St. Elisabeth's church survived lots of disasters with the biggest being the fires in the 1970s. The furnishing of the church got burnt to a great extent then, among other one the most precious organs in Lower Silesia created by a famous organ maker Engler. Nowadays funds have been collected to reconstruct them. However music sounds inside the church. There are concerts within music festivals, among other Forum Musicum, during which musicians perform compositions playing instruments from the epoch, Wratislavia Cantans or Brave Festival.

More than 300 winding and tall stairs lead to a view terrace of the church tower (91 metres high) but the effort is worth making. One can see the panorama of the city from one side there and the Sudetes Ridge from the other. In good weather conditions Śnieżka, the highest peak of the Karkonosze, is visible from there as well.

"Hansel and Gretel" tenement houses

9   Hansel and Gretel

Two picturesque tenement houses, which perfectly seen from the perspective of the fountain in the Main Market Square are "Hansel and Gretel". Both of them called in this way after the war, are former altarists' houses – church service of St. Elisabeth's church and the guard of the former church adjacent cemetery. On the gate linking them there is an inscription "Mors ianua vitae" (Death is a gate of life).

Currently, the Gothic Hansel houses a workshop of a Wrocław copper engraver Eugeniusz Get-Stankiewicz. Above the entrance to the house there is a bas relief – a self-portrait of the artist and at one side there is his provocative work of art entitled "Do it yourself". In the bigger Baroque house there is a seat of Wrocław Lovers Society. It is worth knowing that the vicinity has been enjoyed by dwarfs and behind Hansel the entrance to their settlement is guarded by a dwarf, Halberdier.

Behind the houses one can see a plate footpath running to St. Elisabeth's church. There were the graves of twenty two mutineers. In 1418 they rose against the city council and were punished with death. They

Dwarf the Halberdier guarding the entrance to the settlement of Wrocław dwarfs

were buried on the way to the church so that they would never reach the peace. The following generations, treading upon their graves were to administer the posthumous, severe punishment.

On the former cemetery there is also a statue of an Evangelical theologian, Dietrich Bonhoffer, who was born in Wrocław. He was a participant of the anti-Nazi movement and was killed in a concentration camp in Flossenburg.

10 Old Butchers' Stalls

Butchers' stalls – stalls where meat was sold from medieval times changed their original function after 700 years and became art galleries at the end of the 20th century. Only minor traces have stayed after the old activity of Wrocław butchers. A testimony of the old times in that picturesque corner of the Old City are hatches leading to cool storage rooms which were under the stalls, a lintel of a butcher's house with bas-relief images of a butcher and cattle going to a slaughterhouse. The fact that meat trade was going on here is commemorated by a monument "To Slaughter Animals". There are

The Old Butchers' Stalls

natural sized brass figures of animals made by Wrocław artists on the road paved by field stones. It is since not long ago that an inhabitant of the Butchers Stalls is a butcher – one of Wrocław dwarfs leaning on the door of his stall, holding an axe and protecting his property.

Numerous art galleries which found their place in that narrow street present rich and varied artistic output of local artists. One can buy interesting jewellery, paintings, sculptures, glassware and weaving workshop products. On the stalls there is a marble plate with a mathematical rule "1+1=2". It is a work of a Wrocław artist Eugeniusz Get-Stankiewicz and the title of it is "The Tablet to Simple Rules". It has become a tradition since 1994 that each year its author unveils the plate ceremoniously on 20th of December at 2 p.m.

The monument to "The Memory of Slaughter animals"

THE UNIVERSITY

The main building of the University of Wrocław

11 The University

The building of the University of Wrocław, seen from the side of the River Odra, impresses with its long, ca. 170m, Baroque façade. The building of the University of Wrocław connected to the University church and St. Joseph's boarding school standing next to it create a Baroque corner of Wrocław.

Personifications of the four cardinal virtues (Justice, Valour, Wisdom and Moderation) over the main entrance to the University remind which virtues should be possessed by those who threshold one of the best universities in Poland established by Jesuits in 1702. The door leading to the vestibule are ornamented with Habsburg eagles with the initials of the founder of the University – Emperor Leopold I.

The ground floor houses the Museum of Wrocław University, the college which boasts of a few Nobel Prize winners among its students and professors (among other a doctor Paul Ehrlich, a chemist Fritz Haber, a physicist Max Born). On the right hand side there is Oratorium Marianum, a music room where music world celebrities gave their concerts: Karol Lipiński, Ferenc Liszt, Johannes Brahms, Edward Grieg.

Walking along a grand staircase, the so-called imperial stairs, we cross the whole Silesia symbolically. Over our heads there are allegoric presentations of Silesian duchies with their towns and historical relics. On the first floor on the plafond dedicated to Wrocław Duchy, behind the figure of the just and mighty Wratislavia, we can easily recognize the exposed University building. Wooden doors on the first floor lead to a Baroque treasure of the University: Aula Leopoldina. Walking up the stairs we can reach the Mathematic Tower (formerly there was an astronomical observatory there as the 17th geographical longitude runs through the place) where the terrace allows for observing the city panorama accompanied by personifications of four faculties: Theology, Philosophy, Law and Medicine.

The Mathematical Tower

A statue of a fencer standing on the small square in front of the main building in University Square is a warning to students. It was in this way (naked, only with a sword) that a career of one student came to an end when his artlessness and passion for cards and beer were used by "more experienced" mates.

The Statue of a Fencer,
a fountain on University Square

Aula Leopoldina

11 Aula Leopoldina

Fortunately a representative room of the University of Wrocław, considered to be the most beautful, lay Baroque interior in Lower Silesia was saved during air raids over Wrocław. Thanks to that we can admire a harmonious connection of architecture, sculpture, painting and furnishing. Despite a lay character of the interior one cannot resist a feeling of entering a church. There is nothing strange in it as the College was run by Jesuits according to who earthly knowledge was possible thanks to God's Eternal Wisdom (on the vault of the middle part of the room, God's Eternal Wisdom is presented allegorically as a woman over the head of whom there is a dove – a symbol of the Holy Spirit). On the platform, on the vault one can recognize saints – patrons of Silesia and Wrocław, guardians of the University and Jesuit saints (St. Hedwig of Silesia, St. John the Baptist, St. Leopold, St. Xavier and St. Ignatius Loyola) who entrust the college to God's Mother.

The Jesuits could show their gratitude to earthly authorities as well. The founder of Aula Leopoldina – Emperor Leopold I sits on a throne with a sceptre and a laurel wreath on his head and accompanied by his virtues: Caution and Providence. At the sides of the platform there are his two sons, heirs – Joseph I and Charles VI. The paintings hanging in the auditorium depict those people who contributed to the development of the Jesuit Society and the creation of the University. On the music gallery there is a bust of the most important imperial official in Silesia – Johann Anton Schaffgotsch.

Over the gallery the author of the frescoes, Christoph Handke, painted the proud Silesia (a personification of Silesia) looking towards Emperor Leopold, her daughter – beautiful Wratislavia and the harsh looking god of the River Odra, Viadrus.

12 The University Church

The church dedicated to The Holy Name of Jesus with a modest, compact façade built at the end of the 17th century impresses the visitors with its Baroque interior. A disciple of the famous Andrea del Pozza – a Jesuit Christopher Tausch designed the interior of the church. The high altar and magnificent wall paintings by a Viennese master Johann Michael Rottmayer refer to the dedication of the church and the mission of the Jesuit Society.

A copy of Michelangelo's "Pieta" in the University Church

The painting in the high altar depicts the scenes of presentation in the temple and circumcision (it was during circumcision that Jews gave a name to the child). The frescoes over the presbytery show the Old Testament prophets worshipping the name of Jehovah. Over the main nave the saints and founders of the Jesuit Society adore the Most Holy Name of Jesus placed on a chariot driven and drawn by the evangelists' symbols. The scene is admired from illusive balconies by representatives of four continents and celebrities of contemporary Europe, among other the founder of the University of Wrocław, Emperor Leopold I and the author of the frescoes – Rottmayer. The painter is accompanied by a small dog, which apparently warned the artist against a fall from the scaffolding saving his life in this way.

Apart from various paintings depicting the scenes from the life of Jesus and the lives of saints, an angel orchestra, full of dynamics sculptures of Jesuit saints, Ignatius Loyola and Francis Xavier it is worth to turn your attention to a statue of Our Lady of Sorrows which is a perfect copy of Pieta by Michelangelo Buonarroti.

The University Church, a mirror image in the building of the Faculty of Law and Administration of the University of Wrocław

MARY MAGDALENE'S CHURCH

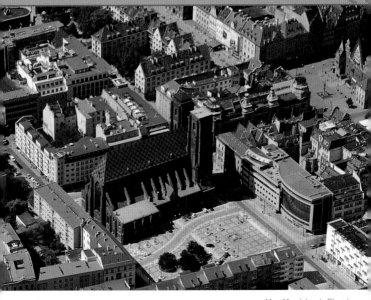

Mary Magdalene's Church

13 Mary Magdalene's Church

A Gothic building from raw brick with two 72-metre-high massive towers proves great ambitions of Wrocław townsmen. The building of the church was begun in the middle of the 14th century. It was a church of rich guilds and craftsmen and there were as many as 58 altars here in the 16th century. Mary Magdalene's Church played a great role in the history of Reformation Period in Silesia. Already in 1523 there was the first protestant service held in the church. The church stayed in Lutheran hands for a few following centuries until 1945. During World War II it was severely damaged. Nowadays it plays the role of a cathedral for the Polish Church.

Outside, at south there is a sandstone Romanesque portal from the 12th century. It was moved here in the 16th century from a pulled down abbey on Ołbin situated on the right bank of the Odra. The portal amazes with a richness of details, scenes from the lives of Mother of God and Christ are depicted on the second archivolt at a small area. Numerous medieval, Renaissance and Baroque epitaphs of Wrocław townsmen are embedded in the walls of the church. Between the towers there is the highest situated footbridge in Wrocław, called the Bridge of Penitent Women. Apparently this is

MARY MAGDALENE'S CHURCH

The towers of Mary Magdalene's Church with the Penitential Women's Bridge also called the Bridge of Witches

the place of penance for the girls who turned down the courtship of young men and never got married. They ran away from the household duties awaiting them after weddings and they have had to clean the bridge ever since.

Inside the church there is one of the most beautiful Wrocław pulpits. The basket supported on the shoulders of angels depicts scenes from the Old Testament carved in alabaster. The presbytery holds a Gothic Sacramentarium with carved scenes of Christ's Passion.

The interior of the church with magnificent acoustics, becomes a concert hall of the International Festival Wratislavia Cantans each year.

The Romanesque Ołbin Portal from the 12th century which is a remnant of the old abbey on Ołbin

The Tumski Bridge and Our Lady's Church on Piasek

14 The Sand Island

The ancient amber route ran through the Sand Island neighbouring with Ostrów Tumski leading from the Adriatic Sea to the Baltic Sea. At the place of nowadays bridges: The Sand Bridge and the Mill Bridge there were the oldest fords across the Odra. The island was inhabited already in the 11th century. In the 12th century it belonged to one of the most powerful Silesian nobles – Piotr Włostowic, who was a very generous man. Foundation of as many as 77 churches and monasteries are attributed to him. The Odra walking boulevard created after the flood in 1997 bears his name.

There were three churches and two monasteries on that small island. One of them, a Gothic church of Blessed Virgin Mary belongs to the biggest churches in Wrocław nowadays. The contemporary building dating from the 14th century was erected at the place of the church founded by Włostowic's wife, Mary. The founding tympanum, which informs that Mary presented the church to Blessed Virgin Mary, can be seen at the entrance to the sacristy. One cannot find any trace of Baroque interior design today as the

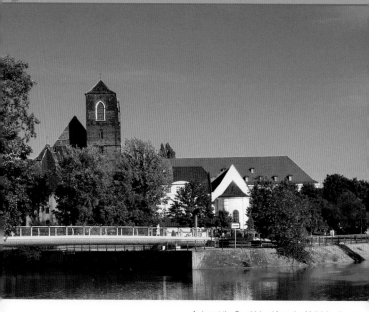

A view at the Sand Island from the Malt Island

church was demolished in 70% during World War II. In the hall interior with the height of almost 23 metres and the width of 80 metres one can see Gothic altars moved from other Silesian churches ones of the best post-war stained glass by Teresa Reklewska and the Miraculous Image of Our Lady of Mariampol accompanying hetman Jabłonowski in the battle of Vienna with the Turks. An attraction for children is a movable nativity which is placed in a side chapel.

A Baroque building adjacent to the church was an Augustine monastery. At the beginning of the 19th century the collections of the University Library were placed there and during World War II it was the headquarters of Festung Breslau. As many as 300 thousand old manuscripts moved to the standing opposite the street St. Anne's Church were devastated during a fire that burst out in May 1945. Nowadays the old monastery houses special collections of the University Library with a collection of 310 thousand old manuscripts and 3 thousand medieval manuscripts.

An Ostrów Tumski panorama from Włostowic's Boulevard

15 Ostrów Tumski

Ostrów Tumski, i.e. the cathedral island is the oldest part of the city. It was here that a stronghold surrounded with a high rampart was established. In the western part of the island the first ducal castle was built. From the 16th century the clergy had their autonomic rule here. The Tumski Bridge, with a coats of arms of the bishop placed on it demarcated a clear border behind which the authority and justice belonged to the bishop. Even dukes crossing the bridge had to take off their hats and town courts could not pursue criminals here.

Despite the fact that after secularization of church estates in 1810 by Prussia, the bishop and the clergy lost their independence on Ostrów Tumski, the place has lived its own rhythm until today. Majority of buildings are taken by the Church related institutions. The archbishop has its seat in a palace at 11 Cathedral Street and beside the palace there is the Archbishop Curia (n°15). Not far away from each other there are a few monastic houses and a hospital run by St. Elizabeth's sisters. There is a Catholic radio here – Radio Family and accommodation is offered by a guest house – John Paul II's House. One can study at two Catholic colleges here: The Metropolitan High Seminary and at the Papal Theological Faculty. An interesting collection of sacral art is shown to the public by the Archdiocesan Museum.

On a small sized old island (in 1824 a fork of the Odra was filled joining the island to the main land from the eastern side) there are five Gothic churches. They differ from each other in size, the time of origin, architectural solutions. The most important of them is certainly the mother of all Wrocław churches – the cathe-

The towers of the Cathedral and of the Holy Cross Church

dral of St. John the Baptist. The oldest church in Wrocław, dating from the beginning of the 13th century and containing some elements of Romanesque architecture, is a small church of St. Giles standing opposite the cathedral. However a harmonious Gothic style with ideal proportions is presented by a double level Holy Cross and St. Bartholomew's Church. There is a Baroque statue of St. John of Nepomuk, one of the most popular saints in Silesia. The Saint is a patron of fathers confessors and it is to protect the island from flooding. The 15th century Sts. Peter and Paul's Church has a unique nave vault supported on one pillar and the small St. Martin's Church is a remain after the old castle chapel.

Ostrów Tumski is not only an oasis of silence and greenery (the Botanical Garden and the bishop's gardens by the Odra) but a place with which the highest number of Wrocław legends are connected. Supposedly it was here that a Polish Prince Mesko, who regained his sight after taking the baptism, waited for his future wife, a Bohemian princess, Dubrawka. On the wall of the south cathedral tower one can find a stone head of a cruel criminal Henry, who was put to custody here for his bad deeds. The Dumpling Gate which is situated beside St. Giles' Church, took its name from Silesian dumplings which a loving wife sent her husband straight from heaven. The gate still has one petrified dumpling attached to it. On the Tumski Bridge, called a "bridge of love" one can meet

the love of his life, it is enough to look carefully into the eyes of passers by.

It is worth coming to Ostrów Tumski in the evening, when gas streetlamps create a unique atmosphere. With a bit of luck one can meet the lamplighter who goes around and makes 90 lanterns glow and puts them out again every day.

The statue of St. John of Nepomuk in front of the Holy Cross Church

Ostrów Tumski – the Cathedral Street, the Cathedral in the background

The cathedral – wall painting in the Baroque St. Elizabeth's Chapel

16 St. John the Baptist's Cathedral

When the bishopric was founded in Wrocław in 1000, there was a stone church at the place of the contemporary cathedral. The present Gothic church, the fourth one there, was erected in stages. The building was started in 1244 after the Mogul's invasion of the city. Almost one hundred years later a triple-aisle basilica with four towers was ready and subsequent chapels were added to it later.

Out of the three entrances to he church the western one with a neo-Gothic portico is most decorative and monumental. The entrance to the church is guarded by stone lions which, according to a legend, can fulfil wishes (one must stroke them tenderly on their tummies). The most precious chapels are behind the presbytery in the altar ambulatory. They became a burial place of their founders, bishops and they were designed by real masters. The builder of the Gothic Our Lady's Chapel was master Pieszko, who worked on, among other, the construction of Our Lady's Church in Cracow. The authors of the Baroque St. Elisabeth's chapel are Italian artists: Giacomo Scianzi, Ercole Ferrata, Domenico Guidi. The Corpus Christi Chapel, called the Elector's chapel was designed by an Austrian Baroque architect Fischer von Erlach.

A statue of St. Elizabeth in the high altar of St. Elizabeth's Chapel

CATHEDRAL

The nave in Wrocław Cathedral

The cathedral turned into ruin during World War II but already in 1951 a Holy Mass was served in the rebuilt church. The furnishing of the church contains a worth noticing Gothic high altar depicting the Dormition of the Blessed Virgin Mary and Baroque stalls with carved scenes of St. Norbert's life. The organ placed here are the biggest in Poland taking into consideration the number of pipes. In the side altar the image of Our Lady of Sobieski which was a gift of the Pope for King John III Sobieski for the victory over the Turks at Vienna. Some people call the figure in the image Our Lady with Moving Eyes as one can have a feeling that Mary's eyes follow the faithful passing the painting.

Climbing the 56-metre-high tower using a lift and one can find himself on a view terrace and admire the panorama of Wrocław.

17 The Archdiocesan Museum

Visiting Ostrów Tumski it is worth entering the museum, which has existed since 1903 and the collection of which possesses objects withdrawn from worship, coming from churches, monasteries, parish priest's houses and gifts from private people. A big collection of Gothic altars, paintings and sacral sculptures, vestments, liturgical objects and artistic craft have been collected here. One

The Archdiocesan Museum

can be surprised by a variety of the presented objects: a natural size statue of St. George on a horse killing a dragon – monster, an Egyptian mummy, plates with cuneiform script, a stone on which there is a miraculously pressed imprint of St. Adalbert's foot. An extremely precious exhibit is a 15th century huge wooden archive cabinet, the so-called Paszkowicz's cabinet. The museum stores the Henry's Book bound in pigskin with the oldest written sentence in Polish. The history of this sentence shows multiculturalism and complexity of the history of Silesia as the sentence was

spoken by Boguchwał, a Bohemian by origin, to his Polish wife and the situation was described naturally in Latin by a German monk.

It is worth turning your attention to an ingeniously set root found during the building of the Holy Cross church. According to a Wrocław legend it was to this root, which resembles a cross in its shape, that the church owes its name.

An exhibition in the Archdiocesan Museum, a statue of St. George on a horse killing a dragon

White water lilies

18 The Botanical Garden

The Botanical Garden, neighbouring Gothic churches of Ostrów Tumski, was created in 1811 as a scientific post of the newly established University of Wrocław.

The garden holds a collection of plants, which contains ca. eleven thousand species, including a lot of monument trees, among other a 120-year-old tulip tree or a maidenhair tree (ginkgo biloba) (they are male and female plants accreted together).

Over 20 petrified tree trunks with the biggest one three metres high and ca. 200 million years old are monuments of nature.

The garden takes the area of 7.4ha gathering plants from all corners of the world, in the palm house we can see tropical and subtropical zone plants, in the cacti house there are over 2.5 thousand species and specimens of succulents, in aquariums there arc fresh water and bog plants. A geological profile of a coal ledge with imprints of extinct plants was built in the alpine plant section in 1856. Behind the alpine area there is a stand of plants which are protected in Poland. A permanent exhibition "Nature Panorama" showing the development of live nature was organized on the area of the garden.

Ponds, small bridges, cascades, open air sculptures and summer Sunday concerts create a unique atmosphere of an oasis of greenery situated in the centre of a city.

There is the Natural History Museum with rich collections of exhibits from the world of animals and plants adjoined to the Botanical Garden. Visitors can see, among other, whales' skeletons and a skeleton of an extinct giant deer.

The National Museum

19   The National Museum

The building housing the National Museum today was erected in 1886. With its architecture it refers to German palace assumptions from the 16th century and to northern renaissance. It is an example of a searching current which was fashionable in the19th century of the so-called "national style" in German architecture.

The Museum can boast of valuable and biggest in Poland collections of medieval art and a big collection of modern art among its over 120 thousand exhibits. The museum rooms and corridors show, among other, burial slabs of the Piast family dukes with a tomb of a Wrocław Duke Henry IV Probus (d. 1290). Medieval sculpture and painting originating from Lower Silesian churches, like e.g. "Mary Enthroned with the Infant on Lions" from Skarbmierz (ca. 1360) have been collected here. The Museum possesses as many as 40 canvas of the master of Polish Baroque, Michael Willman and the biggest in Europe collection of Magdalena Abakanowicz's works. Rich collections of Wrocław Museum are exhibits from various fields of art: painting, engraving, sculpture, craft and ceramics and glassware. Apart from interesting temporary exhibitions there are worth seeing exhibitions that have a permanent character and are devoted to the following subjects: "Silesian stone sculpture of the 12th-16th centuries", "Silesian art of the 16th-19th centuries", "Polish art of the 17th-19th centuries", "Polish art of the 20th century".

The Panorama Racławice Rotunda

20 Panorama Racławicka (The Racławice Panorama)

Only one painting is exhibited in a big, ivy-clad rotunda. It is one 32 existing painting panoramas in Europe. The battle between the Polish uprising army under General Tadeusz Kościuszko and the Russian army led by General Tormasow was fought at Racławice on the 4th of April 1794. A painted vision of the battle fought in the vicinity of Cracow is depicted in a 120-metre-long and 15-metre-high painting taking 1800m² area. The authors and the idea givers were Jan Styka and Wojciech Kossak, who painted the image with the help of other artists in only 9 months. The Panorama was first presented to visitors in Lvov in 1894 on the 100th anniversary of the victorious battle. The painting was damaged during air raids of Lvov in 1944. The partially damaged painting was rolled onto a giant cylinder and moved the Bernardine monastery in Lvov thanks to which it survived the war. It was brought to Wrocław in 1946 but due to a politically incorrect subject at that time its renovation was postponed. The painting underwent conservation work only in the years 1981-1985 and in 1985 it was shown to the public. Until now it has been visited by over 6 million people.

Tadeusz Kościuszko – a part of Panorama Racławicka painting

A part of Panorama Racławicka painting

Looking at the painting from a specially constructed platform it is difficult to discern the border between what was painted on the canvas and the accessory scenes. The illusion is created by lighting and the perfectly arranged space around the image.

Visitors who are particularly interested in the course of the battle may follow the movements of both armies and see the uniforms of soldiers fighting at Racławice in a Small Rotunda. A film concerning other panoramas in the world and the process of renovation of Racławice Panorama can be watched in the hall.

The building of the Museum of Architecture, an old Bernardine monastery

21 The Museum of Architecture

The Museum of Architecture in Poland has existed since 1965. Its seat is a Gothic interior of a former monastery and a church. The history of origin of the place was connected with the activity of St. John Capistrano, a co-founder of the Bernardine Order. St. John Capistrano was appointed the General Inquisitor by Pope Nicholas V against demoralization and heresy. In 1450 he began his six-year-old mission journey during which he preached and established new Bernardine Monasteries. In 1453 he came to Wrocław with a group of 30 friars. The City Council gave him a parcel to build a monastery and already in the year of receiving that gift the Bernardines erected a wooden church at the place. After 10 years they started building the nowadays brick church and monastery buildings. The work on the youngest Gothic church in Wrocław finished in 1517.

Relics, documents, architectural designs, photos connected with old and modern architecture and its creators are collected in the building renovated after World War II damages. The Museum of Architecture recommends seeing the relics of the old abbey on Ołbin with a Romanesque tympanum of Jaksa, coats of arms of Wrocław tenement houses, a rich collection of stained glass and tiles and a model depicting the urban development of Wrocław. Gallery of One Design presents authors' contemporary urban solutions each month.

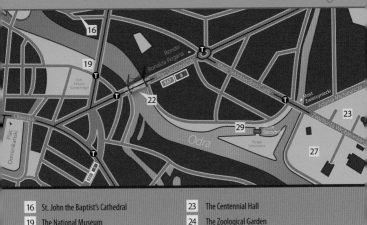

16	St. John the Baptist's Cathedral		23	The Centennial Hall
19	The National Museum		24	The Zoological Garden
22	The Grunwald Bridge		29	The Odra River Museum FOMT

22 The Grunwald Bridge

Wrocław has more than one hundred bridges. A lot of them distinguish themselves with exceptional beauty and picturesque locations. The most famous bridge in the city is the Grunwald Bridge joining the Odra banks, playing a very important role in the communication system of the city. It runs from the left-bank Wrocław into the part of the city where there are a lot of Wrocław colleges.

The bridge has an interesting construction, it is the biggest suspension bridge in Poland. Steel bands are thrown over pylons and anchored in the ground. That apparently light construction weighs 2300 tonnes. Walking over the 112.5-metre-long bridge we pass huge granite gates resembling triumpah arches in their shape.

Historical events had influence on the name of the bridge. Originally it was the Imperial Bridge as the Emperor William II came to Wrocław in 1910 to open it. During the Weimar Republic it was renamed to The Bridge of Freedom. In Polish Wrocław it received the name of the Grunwald Bridge to commemorate the victorious battle of Polish army over the Teutonic Order.

On the one side there is a panorama of Ostrów Tumski and the Sand Island and on the other one can see a historic 19th-century water tower.

The Grunwald Bridge pylons

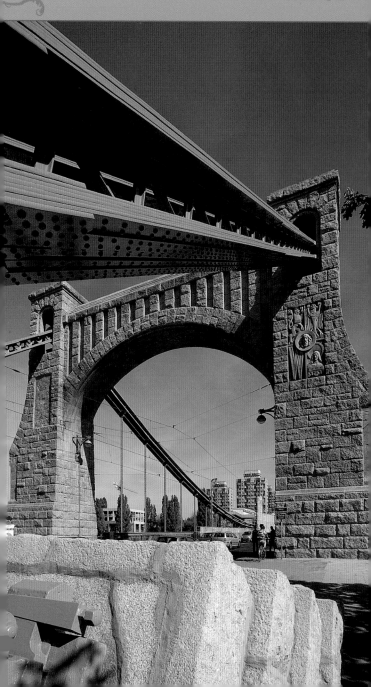

23	The Centennial Hall	**26**	The wooden St. John of Nepomuk'a Church
24	The Japanese Garden	**27**	The Zoological Garden
25	The Szczytnicki Park	**28**	The Spire

23 The Centennial Hall

The Centennial Hall is a symbol and pride of Wrocław. In 2006 it was included in the World Heritage of Culture list of UNESCO although critics of Max Berg's design saw a hat box or a cement birthday cake in its shape. There were also such of them who thought that the dome of the building with a record 65-metre span at that time (the beginning of the 20th century) would certainly collapse.

The opening of The Centennial Hall took place in 1913 and it was connected to a centenary of the Prussian king's, Frederick William III's, appeal to the nation and the victory over Napoleon at Leipzig. A Historical Exhibition was organized in the Four Domes Pavilion, designed by Poelzig, neighbouring the Hall, and the adjoining grounds were embellished with garden art exhibitions.

The Centennial Hall with a pergola

The heir to the throne, Prince William, took part in the opening ceremony of the building and the Nobel Prize winner, Gerhart Hauptmann, wrote a drama "Festspiel in deutschen Reimen" especially for the occasion. A monumental character of that modernistic structure must have amazed people at the beginning of the 20th century: the dome which was 1.5 times bigger than the Pantheon in Rome, the biggest organ in the world – 185 voices, use surface area – 11000m^2, 2400 windows, the interior resembling a Gothic church.

From the assumption the Hall was to fulfil two tasks: it was to be an exhibition interior and a place of gathering. It has played both roles until today. In 1948, during the World Congress of Intellectuals, celebrities of the world of art and culture visited Wrocław. Among other there were: Pablo Picasso, Max Frisch, Aldous Huxley, Michaił Szołochow, Bertolt Brecht. It was here that the future President of Poland, Lech Wałęsa addressed the people of Wrocław and in 1997 Pope John Paul II met the participants of the World Eucharistic Congress. Nowadays fairs, sport and big cultural events take place here (Wrocław Opera Theatre staged, among other, "Aida" by Verdi).

A wooden arch bridge (TAIKO BASHI)

24 The Japanese Garden

Wrocław Japanese Garden is a unique in Europe live part of Japanese culture. It was created within the Garden Art Exhibition, which was a part of the Centennial Exhibition in 1913. The garden was created by the contemporary expert and amateur of Japan, a traveller and collector, earl Fritz von Hochberg and was one of the main attractions of the exhibition. In 1993 a decision to reproduce the old garden solution was undertaken. A team of Japanese specialists took part in the work. All the elements of Wrocław garden are in compliance with the Japanese art of creating gardens. The garden is entered by walking through a wooden gate (sukiyamon), characteristic for Japanese garden art. In the garden there is a tea pavilion (azumaya). Water cascades – an impetuous male one (otoko daki) and a mild female one (onna daki), join together while flowing into a pond. An wooden arch bridge (yumedono) over the pond symbolizes a hard way to reach perfection. At the paths there are stone lanterns and bowls from the Japanese city of Nagoya. There are over 50 species of plants originating from Japan and Eastern Asia. The garden is most beautiful in May when colourful rhododendrons, azaleas and irises bloom.

A fountain by Centennial Hall

25 The Szczytnicki Park

The oldest and the biggest park of the city was created from the garden of the Ducal Governor Prince Friedrich Hohenlohe-Ingelfingen and the green area adjoining the garden. Already in the 18th century the landscape park which was a park of a private garden was open to public.

At the beginning of the 20th century the southern part of the park was designed for exhibition grounds. The Centennial Hall, Four Domes Pavilion and a pergola were built to the needs of the great exhibition in 1913. The Japanese Garden was created within garden art exhibition and the 17th century small St. John's of Nepomuk church was moved there from Stare Koźle in Opole Silesia.

The wooden St. John of Nepomuk's Church in the Szczytnicki Park

Since 1952 the Four Domes Pavilion has been occupied by Wrocław Film Studio, in which such films like: "Popiół i diament" by Andrzej Wajda, "Rękopis znaleziony w Saragossie" by Wojciech Jerzy Has and Polish series: "Czterej pancerni i pies" and "Stawka większa niż życie" were produced. Peter Greenaway shot his pictures to the film "Nightwatching" here in 2006. The pergola in a shape of a horseshoe with the length of over 700 metres situated by a pond with a fountain is a popular place of walks.

On over 100ha area of the park, apart from local species, one can find trees and shrubs coming from, among other, Japan, China, Caucasus, the Balkans and North America. Vast clearings, streams, small footbridges, rhododendron and azaleas gatherings or a rose garden cause that the park is a favourite relaxation and recreation area. A summer cinema is active here in summer and Wrocław Opera Theatre stages its open air performances here as well.

The Szczytnicki Park in autumn

Lionesses

27   The Zoological Garden

Wrocław ZOO, among other 100 zoological gardens in Europe, was created on the wave of Charles Darwin's discovery and publishing a multi-volume work of Alfred Brehm on the life of animals in the second half of the 19th century. Open on the 10th of July 1865 it is the oldest zoological garden in Poland. A large area lying outside the city, limited by the Odra on two sides was ideal to set up a zoo. In the times that the garden originated one had to travel by a horse-drawn omnibus or by ship.

The main gate of Wrocław ZOO

In its over 140-year-long history the garden experienced a lot of dramatic events. It was closed for the first time during the economic crisis of the 1920s and later only 200 animals survived the cataclysm of World War II. The garden was liquidated at that time. The zoo restarted its activity in 1948. The renaissance of the Zoo was in the

THE ZOOLOGICAL GARDEN

Elephants

1950s. The area of the garden was increased from 13ha to 30ha and scientific-farming work began.

The garden started its activity in the 19th century with only 189 animals while today it can boast of the biggest in Poland collection of over 4000 animals which belong to over 600 species. A lot of them are protected species or the ones that are not encountered in the natural environment any more.

The place was included in the list of the relic register as on the grounds of the ZOO there are buildings from the end of the 19th century. There are the birdhouse, an elephant pavilion and a monkey house. The old restaurant hoses a terrarium now. Flora in Wrocław Zoo is worth noticing as well because there are exotic dendrologic specimens growing there.

Baboons

1:10 000 (1cm -100m)

100   50   0   500

H	Hotels
P	Car parks
WC	Toilets
🍴	Gastronomic points
🏄	Sport and tourist wharves
⚓	Passenger ships wharves
⚓	Harbours

11	The University
44	Clare'Weir
45	The Malt Footbridge (Most Słodowy)
46	Maciej's Weir
47	The hydro-electric plant Wrocław I
48	The Townsfolk Sluice
49	The hydro-electric plant Wrocław II
50	The Old Town Harbour
51	The W. Sikorski Bridge

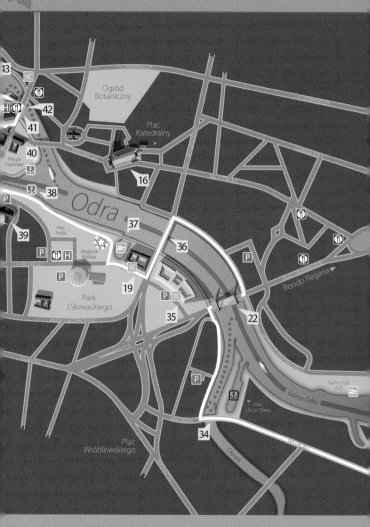

Rondo Regana

Stara Odra

Górna Odra

Yacht Club
AZS

Wyspa
Szczytnicka

Relaks

Port
Ujście Oławy

Oława

NAD ODRĄ

Ogród
Zoologiczn

WUPR

22
29
30
31
32
33

22	The Grunwald Bridge
29	The Odra River Museum FOMT
30	The Zwierzyniecki Bridge
31	The Zwierzyniecka Wharf
32	The Zwierzyniecka Footbridge
33	The Szczytnicki Weir

- P━━K A walking and cycling path
- Additional pieces of the walking and cycling path
- Scenic points along the route
- The Water Route – the beginning and the end
- Additional pieces of the water route
- Portages

River Fleet ships at the Cardinal's Wharf

Venice of the North

„Venice of the North" – to understand why Wrocław has got that name it is enough to look at the city from the river perspective, or rather the perspective of the rivers that flow through it. The Odra with its four tributaries: the Oława, the Ślęza, the Bystrzyca and the Widawa flows around a dozen of city oslands. Bridges and footbridges spanning over Wrocław waters, they amount to more than one hundred, create picturesque corners and a unique climate of the city.

Wrocław water knot has been formed through centuries to take its current form in the 1920s. It is a unique hydro-technical object along which there goes a tourist route called "Technological Relics of Wrocław City Centre Water Knot" to be best visited by bike. The city may be looked at from the river perspective during White Fleet river cruises organized regularly in summer (from the beginning of April until the end of October) which are one of tourist attractions of Wrocław. The cruises start at three points, the Zwierzyniecka pier at the ZOO which is slightly away from the city centre, and two other points situated close to the Old Town. Those are the Cardinal's Pier at Włostowic's Boulevard and the Trade (Targowa) Pier at the Trade Hall.

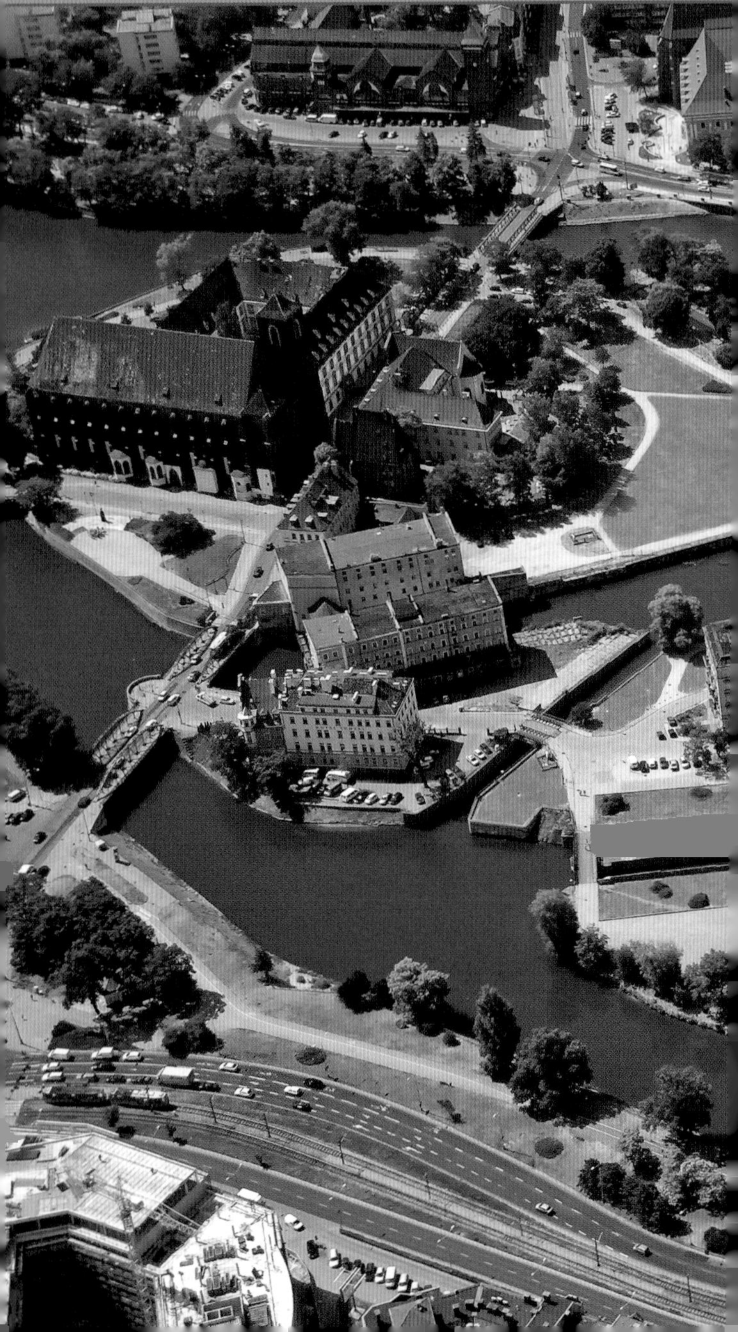

The Main Railway Station

The Main Railway Station and the Świebodzki Railway Station

It was in 1846 that Wrocław could boast of a railway connection with Berlin. A dynamic development of railways in the first half of the 19th century caused that three railway stations were built in Wrocław within only three years: Górnośląski (Upper Silesian) (1842), Świebodzki (1843) and Dolnośląski (Lower Silesian) (1844).

In 1855 the inhabitants of Wrocław received a new, more developed Górnośląski Railway Station – the nowadays Main Railway Station. The former did not fully satisfy the needs of a growing city. It is hard to believe that the railway station that is situated in the very centre of the city now, was on the outskirts of it when it was created. It was then surrounded by a garden and farm fish ponds which is now proved by street names only: Stawowa (Pond Street), Gliniana (Clay Street), Sucha (Dry Street).

The magnificent building, designed by Wilhelm Grapow in the English Tudor Gothic style with a 200-metre-long hall, belonged to the

The Świebodzki Railway Station

biggest railway stations in Europe once and had three waiting rooms for passengers of the 1st, 2nd and 3rd classes, a big restaurant, apartments for special guests, a lavishly decorated conference room. The representative main entrance was a place of welcome and farewell ceremonies.

During World War II cement storage rooms and air raid shelters were built underground of the square in front of the station and their highest floor is now used as a place of trade.

An equally interesting place architecturally is the building of the old Świebodzki Railway Station. It owes its present appearance to rebuilding in the years 1868-1874. It is palace architecture in Italian Renaissance and Classicist style. Pomerania and Silesia allegories over the main entrance were to symbolize a railway connection to Szczecin. Over the northern entrance one can see allegories of Mercury (a god of trade) and Industria (a goddess of industry). The station does not play its original role now and houses the Polish Theatre, a restaurant and shops inside.

CONTENTS

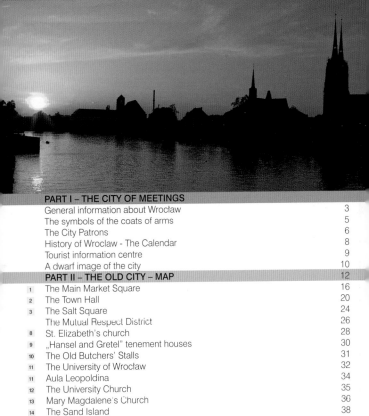